Burgundy Love

A Poetic Conversation
(Revised)

Original Works Written By

I0162085

Navarro Love

N
NAVARIA
Productions

Ne
NAVARIA ENTERPRISES

Navaria Productions
Copyright © 2014 Navaria Enterprises
Registered, WGAw No. 1499009

This is a work of fiction. The events and characters described herein are imaginary and are not intended to refer to specific places or living persons. The opinions expressed in this manuscript are solely the opinions of the author and do not represent the opinions or thoughts of the publisher.

Burgundy Love, A Poetic Conversation
All Rights Reserved.
Copyright © 2014 Navaria Enterprises and Navaria Productions

This book may not be reproduced, transmitted, or stored in whole or in part by any means, including graphic, electronic, or mechanical without the express written consent of the publisher except in the case of brief quotations embodied in critical articles and reviews.

Navaria Enterprises.
http://www.facebook.com/NavariaEnterprises
Twitter: @NavariaEnt
ISBN: 978-0692226544
Navaria Enterprises/Navaria Productions and the "Ne" logo are trademarks belonging to Navaria Enterprises.

PRINTED IN THE UNITED STATES OF AMERICA

Intro

Definition of Burgundy

If you were a color, what would it be? Some say that ones essence can be found within their dreams and imagination. What makes some dream in color and others black and white? If there were a color within the spectrum that would encompass all emotions and feelings what would that color be? The answer I give you is burgundy. The color burgundy holds the key to a door to which behind it resides a wide array of emotions and feelings. No other color can create a backdrop for so many things we all feel and hold dear. Some feelings we cannot hide from some we search and long for. What is the color of love? What is the color of sorry or pain? Some colors are said to reflect a feeling of happiness and bliss others the opposite.

For example why is the color blue accepted as the one true color for sadness? Why does yellow portray cowardice, white purity and black a form of darkness and evil? If all of these colors hold the definition of those feelings and or characteristics then why not burgundy as the beginning and ending of all spiritual, superficial, and emotion feelings that make up the DNA of love, life, happiness and sadness?

I have offered to you my theory. Now here lies the proof. An example. Imagine a room filled with candles and a burning fire.

Each candle the color burgundy, the color on the walls also burgundy. Two lovers share a plate of fruit as they cuddle close together wrapped in a blanket covered in a sea of deep burgundy colored rose petals. This would be the perfect setting for an intimate night of love, romance and lovemaking. This is a not so far left extreme of what love and romance would entail. With that said now for another example totally different in feeling but the backdrop the same.

A man sits alone in his room. Quiet and still he sits thinking of the one he lost. Soft jazz plays in the background as he stares at his four walls of solitude. The room is a dull shade of burgundy. In his hands he holds a photograph of his lost lover. The light of his candle glaring off the glass frame reflects the shade of the walls bringing him deeper into his world of loneliness. Again two different scenarios both accentuated by one color, burgundy. Why burgundy? Just as love has so many different extremes it can be happy one day and very sad the next. Burgundy can reflect all of those emotions, whatever you feel burgundy can bring to life those emotions locked within you. Tell your lover, no longer will our portrait of love be stained with the dull color of red but in fact it will be highlighted with the romantic and sensual color of Burgundy. And from this moment on we will share a love like no other; it's A Love Burgundy.

Acknowledgements

God, our journey has been long and yet we still walk together. Thank U. Mother my love for you has no end. Grandmother, I miss U. Thank you for believing and 4 your unconditional love and support. Friends & family, thank u. To all those I have met in life 4 whatever reason it was meant to be at that particular time. I hold no grudges to those who are no longer around but I can still say F you with a smile. 4 those who are, my love is yours. For all the laughter and good times. Thank U. Be loved and blessed.

Navarro Love

Word from the Writer

Burgundy Love should not be taken as just a book of poetry. Instead it should be seen as a conversation between a man and woman. It is a telling story of what one man feels for one woman and what obstacles they face while traveling that road called monogamy.

Table of Contents

Chapter 1: *Love & Romance*

Chapter 2: **SEX**

Chapter 3: Pain

Chapter 1

Love &

Romance

Genesis Of Love / What is Love?

What is this word love? Four letters that mean so much to some but creates fear for others. What is it about? Is it a treasure lost that so many seek or a disease that some wish to have a cure for? Can anyone tell me? How does it work? What makes one love someone else? Is it really love when one person feels that they are quote "in love"? Can you truly love someone that doesn't love you? So many questions, I guess only experiences can answer. When you feel yourself caught in that matrix called love and you are hurting because you cant be with the one you want has love come to and end? Does love have an end? Can love be created and then destroyed by ones actions? And if it can, was it really love? Life has so many twists and turns and along that road there are three pit stops that everyone will visit. Love will be the first we explore. When a woman says to a man those three words "I Love You", I believe that something deep within her really feels that she is in fact in love. And there's nothing sweeter to that woman than the moment her man replies back to her with "I love you too". Isn't it wonderful to share the most intimate of emotions with someone? To love someone is to bring them close to your soul, your center. My definition of love some may disagree with but one can argue that each person feels the love of someone else in many different ways, here's mine.

Love or shall we say true love is without heartache or pain. The only pain felt is the pain of missing someone for they are not around. Love is created by two not one. One person can't be in love for it takes two individuals to create or make up the nucleus of what love is. Love has no end for it was meant to last forever. Love is respect and understanding, and if you truly love someone those two things will never be mishandled. Love is truth, faith, and unselfishness for it has no lies and the belief is strong and your mates well being and life means more to you than that of your own. To all my ladies, never mistake a man's physical interest for love. To all my fellahs never mistake a "Jones" for having love for a woman. Recognize it for what it is and be honest with yourself and how you feel for that woman because when it ends and she is no longer there that Jones will come. And when that Jones hits, damn, it's a muthafuckah. True love is free, true love is flowing. Love is of course after all burgundy.

A Rose

Navarro Love

I dreamt of a Rose, so delicate so sweet
Though I cried as I awoke, for my dream wasn't complete.
I dreamt of heaven, in the form of you.
A rainbow you are my love, different colors, shades, hues.
I wish to be your eyes so I may see what beauty sees
Would it be things I couldn't understand, things I could never
believe.
Touch me Love, mold me in2 the man God wants me to be.
For with you I am not afraid, for you are my destiny.
And if I should die in your arms, I only have one wish
That I may return as one of your tears, so that I may gently roll
down your cheek
And find my rest upon your lips.
I dreamt of a Rose so vivid, so true
In my darkest hour my love, my voice calls only to you.
Who says a man can't Love, that which is only in his dreams
But in love with you I am my dear, yet your face is unseen.
I dreamt of a Rose, so faithful this is true,
Could the Rose I dream be a Rose that blooms within you?

Descend

Navarro Love

My heart and my flower, my shining light within my darkest hour
To you I descend like an angel on gifted wings
For it were you who entered my heart, and taught me to love again
For you I will learn to fly to the heavens then descend
And I will protect you with all the being of my soul
For I was destined to be your guardian man
Touch my soul and reveal what life's plan has in store for me.
With you I will walk this journey with pride no matter what that
future may be.
Would it be blasphemy to say that I would rather give up a
week in heaven, just for a day with you?
A small thing to ask when your love is real, and everything about
you is truth.
When we embrace it is as if the heavens cry down on us,
and the wind becomes still.
Time has no hold on you and I, although it passes it leaves no
trace.
The only thing that is relevant is the gleam in your eye, and the
look upon your face.
I am here my love to save you from so many heartaches of the past.
Take my hand and fly with me, and let's create a love that will
forever last.
To you I come with open arms willing to embrace the love that is
before me
I have thrown aside all that is of this world and live only for the
love of you
For eternity my heart will forever cherish thee with every breath
that I breathe.

Question Of You

Navarro Love

So tell me the answer, to the question of you.
Shall I give my thoughts; tell me what shall I do.
I've given you everything, even that which matters most,
Still there is no answer, still I find myself lost.
Shall I build a cathedral to you layered in precious stones?
Tell me what do you wish for, either diamonds or gold.
Is there an answer, to the desires within your heart?
So many questions to answer, my love this test is too hard.
So I guess I have failed to answer, the question of you
But I love you just the same, for the answer to my loneliness
still remains
I ask myself, how do u answer the question, of one so bold.
And one who holds the secret, to a love untold.
What shall I answer if ever there was an answer to be made?
My mind becomes cloudy with each breath I take.
In my mind I uncover layer upon layer until suddenly it has
come to me,
The answer I have searched,
like a hidden chord, a missing key.
If I am to answer, I shall answer with a kiss
for a kiss tells no lies, and it reveals to me this.
As you look into my eyes this lonely shade of gray,
Beyond your eyes I see pain of lovers past,
Love often hurt, chaos ran astray.
If I am wrong, still my answer shall stay.
If this is not true, what is the answer to, The Question Of
You?

Heaven

Navarro Love

I've seen you in my dreams
So alive, so vivid they seem.
I long to be close to you like a child to his mother
There's nothing more in this world for me,
For we were made for one another
I think of how beautiful it would be
Just to be in your existence.
There's no journey too far, for you I will travel
any distance.
Heaven, I wish for many things, most of all
to dwell within you.
And when this lonely life's trips is over, I pray that
my wish will come true.
For now I will continue to dream, and dream I will.
Until the day I am within you, for with you
my heart is filled.
Many are skeptical they question the unseen
But my love for you still remains
With every part of my being
Heaven I will continue to dream,
Until the day you and I have met,
For this soul you have captured, without a snare or a net.

2Gether

Navarro Love

"As you and I lay 2gether, I see a future with you and no other,
I wish that you and I would remain 2gether, forever"
You're my heart, you're my soul
You're my flesh you make me whole
Every touch and every breath
That I breathe, my minds at ease
You're my priest, to whom I confess my sins.
And our love shall never end
I will walk with you, till the end of time 2gether
You're the cheek that I kiss. You're the touch upon my lips
Every hour of everyday, I have you on my mind so many words to say.
Come with me, my dear take my hand.
You're my love, and I am your man.
I wait for the day we walk down that aisle 2gether.
You rescue me from my dreams, the nightmares inside haunting me.
With your tears please erase my past,
With each one cleansing me they are my bath.
You're the love I'm reaching for, it's drowning me, I can't ignore.
Inside our arms baby I wish to melt 2gether.
When the cold winters come, whom shall I hold?
Can I call on you? For you have my soul.
I need you, I love you, I reach for you, I am you.
You're the love I'm reaching for. It's drowning me, I can't ignore
Inside our arms, I wish to die 2gether.

My Sanctuary

Navarro Love

I will love you until all of my days are gone past,
And my heart will forever be yours like sand to an hourglass.
Like the wind that blows, a gentle breeze through the leaves
of a tree
You are muse you are my sanctuary.
Would it be wrong of me to say, that in the after life I wish
not to know you
For I have heard that there are no lovers in heaven so what
am I to do?
My soul and being are at rest when I'm with you,
Your presence brings a calm to me, like a field of flowers
after a summers bloom.
Can I love you in silence, and breathe life into your dreams
Can I give you mine in exchange, for you I'd give anything.
Sanctuary divine, like an aged old wine
This is too right to be wrong, for I have spoken to God and
yes, you are rightfully mine.
When this world is too much for me, you are who I hold,
I seek your wisdom, your love, the strength of one so soft yet
bold
I bask in the light, the light that shines from your smile
The warmth of your touch, your healing spirit like a mother
and child.
If our love was a church I seek communion with you
For the sanctuary of my soul, I taste of your blood and life,
and give all that is due.
Lets plant a seed, and as it grows we
will live off the fruit of our tree
And I will love you in truth and in silence, for you are my
sanctuary.

The One

Navarro Love

Today I saw The One
or at least so I thought
Warm as the Sun her smile went through me
Filling the void of space within
For a moment silence, then a gust of wind
I thought I saw The One today
nameless, but what's in a name
I can call her rose or moon
The glow of light she brings lights any room
I thought, I did, I hope she is The One
Cause my heart cant take another false dream
could she be my sun,
stars, moon my everything
A nameless face, her smile devoid of sorrow
I thought I saw The One today,
If not, maybe tomorrow

& God Created Woman

Navarro Love

In the beginning there was Man, but he was nothing without
you
Flowing black hair sensual lips, a face of beauty its true.
Made to be as one, never the bond shall break
Like an oceans abound waters that run into a lake.
Always plentiful is the love the two of them shall share,
And that woman shall never be alone, for her burdens that
man will bare.
To Love and to Protect are his only desires.
The two shall live a life eternal, never a dull flame, 4 their
love is a raging fire.
A man is nothing without the loving spirit of his lady.
For she was born of his body knowing one day she would
have his baby.
My lady, my lover, my friend, my life
From birth we were linked together as husband and wife.
In the beginning it was written, that you should belong to me,
Without you I am a slave, for you set me free.
And we shall die 2gether, only to be reborn again.
Your worth and beauty going un-noticed is certainly a sin.
God created you, for one purpose, to show man the meaning
of truth.
Purity at its best, personified in you

Burgundy Love

Navarro Love

Can I walk a sandy beach with you, and count the many
footprints we've left in the sand.
I swear you give me butterflies with each touch of your hand.
Lets lie in a field of flowers, and reminisce on our past memories.
And listen to a slow flowing stream, as we lay quietly.
Baby you've got my heart, for all my days I pray we last
no we should never part.
To your pain I will be your hurt.
And if presented with a cup of love
Please allow me to drink first.
For that cup is filled with the essence of you,
And forever it quenches my thirst.
Tell me have you ever experienced a love, the color burgundy
It is a love like no other, one devoid of all frailty.
A love created with the soul of man and the essence of woman in
mind.
No words can explain this love, so complex so divine
Purity at its best none are worthy enough to define.
Come with me to a place and in this place only secrets are taboo
Filled with the shade of love, too dark to be blue.
I offer you heaven, heaven locked within my heart,
Say you'll follow me, and forever we shall never part.

Then Came You

Navarro Love

I was cold as a Minneapolis winter, the word love
I really never knew what it was, never really cared.
Then my heart struck a flame like a burning cinder,
when once through my door you entered.
I was skeptical about love, but then came you.
A stranger to what my heart felt, but I refused to let this
frozen heart melt, but then came you.
Suddenly I realized all the games and lies couldn't count
up to the many sparkles in your eyes.
The world I once knew stopped turning and my heart started
burning, once you entered the room.
Once in your presence, I felt heaven for a few seconds
And the man I once knew I knew no more.
For he is locked away in solitude and you hold the key to that
door.
Forever I am entranced with thee, a student of yours my love
teach me.
Teach me to love, to live, to breathe, to sing,
to bask in the joy that is you.
And I will sing all the praises that you are so overdue.
For I was half a man without even knowing
destined to live life alone,
Then came you.

Your Eyes

Navarro Love

If your eyes could sing,

tell me what would I hear

Would it be a sweet serenade meant only for my ear?

I see so much when I gaze upon your eyes

Most of all I see innocence, a figure devoid

of lies

Truth personified within the look of you

So amazing to be loved you've shown

me so much anew

Many have glanced, some given a chance

2 look upon those eyes fixed on your desire

Melting from the warmth, your eyes burn with fire

I wish to make love to you

And look deep within your eyes

To read your emotion as your eyes never lie.

Innocence and praise, one you possess one you deserve

I am yours my love I am here to serve

Just give me one wish, that is all that I ask

Let me gaze upon those eyes of yours

Just for a moment if 4ever should not come to pass.

You Are
Navarro Love

You are my sunshine
when I am blue
You are my rain after a drought
that is long over due
You are my heaven, the laughter
within my dreams
You are my northern star
so close but yet so far
You are my rock
I hold to in a storm
You are my ray of light
in winter you keep me warm
You are my center
To which everything gravitates and flows
You are my heart beat,
my pulse and my soul
You are forever
If never is too much to ask
That by my side you should stay
In the morning when I awake
Your smile always begins my day

The Tears in Your Eyes

Navarro Love

If the sky should ever fall, baby I wouldn't care at all

cause love you thrill me.

If the morning should never come,

I wouldn't care as long

as I spent the night in your arms

And for the tears in your eyes, baby I would surely die

Which means I would love thee.

To your rain I am your wet, let us love forever and live not one

regret

And heaven shall open its doors for us,

As long as we believe and always trust

Trust in our hearts and one another, that the tears that we shed

will bring us closer together.

Baby my bond is in blood with thee, lets make a vow that would

last eternity

Lets build our sanctuary devoid of lies,

And only in happiness will you cry,

And believe in your man, of whom to be I strive

And my love will wipe the tears from your eyes.

Remember my love, that for you I would die

If that would erase the tears from your eyes

The Light

Navarro Love

There's a light in darkness
You can see it there
They say the saviors coming
I hear whispers in the air
It's the greatest feeling
Love covers all the earth
Made to be a ruler, from the day
Of his birth
Some say you can't believe
In that which is not seen
No need to run from heaven
There's nothing to fear
For in your darkest hour
The light will appear
And his face you can behold
The greatest love story ever told
Walk into the light

Journey Through Love (My Evolution)

She was everything a man could hope for. Someone most men see in their dreams. She was beautiful. Hazel eyes, a gorgeous smile and body that would make any man sing. But of course I was young and naïve. Thinking all the while I wanted more than what she was giving at the time. Now in retrospect I see that all the things I was out in the streets searching for I had in her. After a long day at work I would come to her and always a smile would adorn her face. If I needed my back rubbed she would be more than happy to oblige me. If I needed my head scratched, my hair washed or braided she took pride in doing that for me.

Just because she enjoyed my time, no strings attached. Love in its most rare of forms, unconditional. For years that's how it went. Of course we shared our ups and downs, ins and outs, but through it all we remained together. I must admit it was heaven on earth. Though at the time I felt that I was missing out on something. Was it something that I wanted that she couldn't provide or was it just my selfish nature taking hold of me.

Through self-assessment I can say that it wasn't that she couldn't provide or that she was missing out on some mysterious characteristic to keep my interest. But alas it was me who was lacking. Lacking the fundamental truth of being able to recognize a good woman. I can say that now because my mind has elevated to a plain that no longer relies on physicality to keep my interest but now with age I have gained maturity. I now possess the maturity to recognize my weaknesses and my flaws. Everyone has their brand of bullshit that they bring into a relationship but maturity will help you to recognize what brand you are trying to sell. Back then I was always in search of the B.B.B (bigger better booty). Love, hell who cared? It didn't mean much to me. I knew she cared for me or by her admission she loved me but it didn't reflect within my actions or me. Now that I am older, mentally older I have thrown away my childish ways and I welcome love in all its forms. I dream of it, I long for it, I believe in it. My evolution has brought me to a place to where I can recognize truth.

To my ladies I would like to share this. Many of you ask how does a man define a quote "good woman". The answer is simple. A good woman is one that can recognize a "good man". His actions speaks volumes his words the truth. Search yourself and ask when you have come across someone, were you able to recognize that man as a good man and hold on to him or did something within you allow yourself to miss out on the best opportunity of your life. People we must break the cycle. Let go of all the bullshit fallacies of what we consider to be THE ONE.

Tu Solo To

(My Pledge)

Navarro Love

Your style and grace calls me to you

The things you wear accentuate

the lines of your body

Creating a silhouette enticing its true

Your ambition is intriguing to me

I wish to live within your dreams

Yours goals I will help to accomplish

Your stepping-stone I will be

Your smarts and intellect

I crave to know more

I want to massage your mind with mine

And make love to your very soul

Passion, seven letters but it

means so much

A glimpse of your spirit I felt

with just your touch

If the fear of God is what makes you believe

Then I will follow you

for your existence is enough to make me see

And for your love there's nothing on earth

I wouldn't do

Baby, for Tu Solo Tu

Chapter 2

SEX

3SUM

It was about 1am I was at the club. The "shake junt" as I would call it but to most the strip club. It's a little hole in the wall joint with nasty bathrooms and bottom of the barrel chicks. Well don't get me wrong the chicks are okay but the drinks are even better. I had been there about an hour or so got on a few drinks and the night was getting so lame. After my fifth shot of Bacardi I was ready to call it a night then she walked in. She caught my eye from the door, redbone, slim waist pretty face and a big ass just like I like it. After being in the club damn ear all night looking at these low class chicks with bullet wounds and stretch marks I welcomed a change of scenery.

I see her walked through the door and with the first opportunity I made sure that she knew I was watching. I gave her a quick glance but made sure to make eye contact before looking away. I'm thinking to myself "damn this chick is badd"; she proceeds to walk right past my table. I quickly sit up in my chair trying to wipe the half drunk look off my face I straighten my cloths and begin to give her "The Look". Now you may be wondering what is "The Look"? Cant quite explain it but it's a subtle glance with direct eye contact that lasts for maybe 3 to 5 seconds. Although it only lasts a short while it is very powerful if done correctly. And yes I have mastered it. My shit always works. Its like kryptonite to Superman, even the strongest fall victim to it. SO as I'm giving her the look she sits at the table right next to mine all the while not breaking eye contact but only for a second to make sure she doesn't fall flat on her ass. The club closes in about another hour so I don't have much time the flirting begins.

We begin with a bit of smiling which then leads to a quick wink back and forth. I smile at her she winks at me. Right then and there I knew I had her. As I said before "The Look" always works. Like a game of chess, check mate. Now maybe it was all the drinks I had or the little bit of kush I smoked but I didn't notice this older guy sitting next to her. Now she wasn't young but this guy looked to be ten years her senior. Of course I'm not one to judge another man but damn this guy was mediocre at best. He couldn't possibly be with this goddess of a woman I'm thinking to myself. Screw it, I said. I got back into my zone. To make sure that all this flirting wasn't for not, I tried an old school move that would always give away if the chick were really feeling me. The patented get up from the table move. Only real players would know what that means. But for you guys that need help I will be more than happy to share with you what this move is all about. If you are at the club and for some reason you are digging on a chick but you want to make sure that she is feeling you just as much. Get up from your table and walk to the bar or the restroom making sure that you walk directly past her table en-route. While you make your way to the bar or whatever your destination may be, don't look at her at all. Have your homeboy watch her most will become intimidated that you are looking at them and they may try to look away. Now while you homeboy watches her he's looking to see if her eyes follow you the entire time you are en-route to the bar or restroom, if so she wants you but you have to play it right. Otherwise you could mess up the mood and what comes out of your mouth could make or break the deal.

Anyway, after making my trip, of course it worked, I get back to my seat and I'm back at it again. The smiling and flirting right now I know she's all in. Besides the walk to the bar allowed her to get a better picture of the total package. I look over at her and she tips her glass to her lips and winks again. Confirming that in fact the package was nice.

All of sudden over the loud speak I hear "Its time for platter". I wont go into what that means but for you lames, that's my queue to leave. As I get up to leave I notice she is writing something on a piece of paper. No doubt she must be writing down her number to give to me so I stall a little to give her time. After watching these chicks trot on and off stage I'm thinking to myself this night wont be a total waste of time. After a moment of procrastinating I proceed to walk to the door and suddenly she walks up behind me. She gets so close I can feel her wide hips sway from side to side bumping into my side.

Of course I'm not tripping at all this is what I have been waiting for. She doesn't bother to introduce herself she just says "Hello". I respond back in the deepest, sexiest voice I can muster at the time with, "Hello, how are you"? The brief exchange of small talk opens the door for what she says next. She gets closer and whispers in my ear, "Today is my birthday and my husband is willing to fulfill any fantasy I have." I draw back just a little and she gets even closer to me and says. "And tonight my fantasy is to fuck you". Now I'm no square but this is the first time a woman this bad has come with a line so direct and blunt without me having to seduce her first. I try to say something cool but words leave me. I pause for a moment, which seemed like forever before responding with, "Your place or mine?" She tells me to call her and it must be tonight. We both reach the exit of the club and she kisses me on the neck and gets a quick feel of my somewhat erect member. Again words leave me. I respond with a quick but affirmative 'I will call you". In shock and somewhat disbelief I rush my homeboy to the car and begin to tell him about what this chick just said to me.

Of course I'm no stranger to picking up women at the club but the realization that the older guy with her was her husband threw me. And yes, it cut right through my buzz. I open the piece of paper she gave me and it reads a number and name, Dynasty.

Wow, what a name. Whether or not it was her real name was not my concern but all sorts of thoughts were going through my head. One in particular I couldn't shake. I'm thinking to myself, maybe it's a setup. Maybe the older guy with her was gay. Maybe she wants to drug me and while I'm out this guy will try to screw me. That's not how I want my night to end. Begin dumped off by some chick and her old fuck boy is not my idea of fun. I talk to my homeboy to assess the situation before making the call. I'm saying to myself, this could be the best night of my life or the worst. And I don't want to experience the latter.

This I can't shake. This goddess of a woman just gave me the proposal of a lifetime, should I or shouldn't I? The thought of disease damn. What the fuck? I surely don't want that. I think for a moment then shake it off. I get my shit together and make the call. I dial, the phone rings a few times then a voice answers "Hello". I quickly say, "What's up? This is of course Navarro". She replies with a simple "I know". My first question to her is, "Are you for real?" Soon after all my concerns melt away as I'm caught up in this smooth sexy, sensual voice on the other end of the phone. Another question, "So where's your husband?" She responds, "He's right here. We share everything." Without hesitation I quickly make it known, "You muthafuckas won't be sharing me!" We laugh for a moment before she says, "He's cool. Would you like to speak to him"? I let her know that my concern isn't with what he wants to do at this point, but more so about what I want to do with her. I let her know I'm down and proceed to make my way to her side of town after she provides directions.

Even though I'm about to blow this chick's back out I'm still thinking this could possibly be a setup. "Don't take any drinks from her", I remind myself. And just for the sake of piece of mind I take my homeboy Ralph out there with me. The ten-minute drive lasts damn near an hour finally I reach my destination. I pull up to a huge 3-story house. All the lights are out except for one in the upper portion of the house. In all honesty it looks like something out of a horror movie. Before I leave my ride I tell my homeboy to stay alert. Oh and I definitely let him know that if anything crazy pops off come through the door blasting. I check my phones to make sure all batteries are juiced before getting out of the car. I get out and walk to the door, before I can ring the bell the door opens and there stands Dynasty. She stands there wearing a silk robe with nothing underneath. Damn, she looks good. We greet with a simple hello and smile. Still flirting even though I am now standing in her home. She thanks me for coming then takes me by the hand and leads me through her house. Let the games begin! It's a nice house I notice the expensive furniture in the living room. The crystal wine glasses in the kitchen. Nothing cheap about this chick, either she or the old guy makes a lot of money. As she leads me through the house I'm checking out her frame. Her sexy walk is turning me on enough and I haven't even seen her completely naked yet. She looks back at me and offers me a drink. I without hesitation respond with "No, I'm fine." We walk up the back stairway to what I'm assuming leads to her bedroom. As we reach the top I see the flicker of candlelight coming from a back bedroom. I also hear the sound of soft jazz playing. We reach the room and she opens the door. The sound becomes clearer. Soft contemporary instrumental jazz plays, while the room is peppered with candles.

Off in the distance I see a video camera and I that's confirmation enough for me that this is not her first time. She asks if I am comfortable before leaning back on her bed. I stand next to her for a moment then almost out of nowhere the old guy appears. The shit was scary the guy comes out of a secret passage way or something in their house I didn't see him coming. He comes over to me and shakes my hand before thanking me for coming. All the while a smile on his face, I'm thinking damn, what's the catch? I'm waiting on more people to jump out of the closets or something and tell me its all a prank. For the life of me I cant remember the old guys name, but he asks me if I found the house with no problems. I respond with a smooth "yes" before requesting to use the restroom. I go in and immediately I'm texting Ralph. By this time it's almost 4am and I know he has probably fallen asleep. I wait for a minute and I get no response. I look at myself in the mirror and say, "fuck it, its game time". I convince myself it's going down, but if the old guy touches me, I'm blasting him.

I come out of the restroom and Dynasty is sitting on the

bed. She slides down off the bed and walks over to me. She begins to kiss me and out of the corner of my eye I see her husband standing by the dresser working the video camera. She slowly slips off my shirt and our kissing turns to touching. She takes my belt buckle in her hands and loosens it. Unzipping my pants she slides then down and then proceeds to get down on her knees. At this point its like a game of Texas hold 'em. I'm all in! She starts sucking my half erect penis slowly and I can feel it getting harder in her mouth. With each stoke of her lips and tongue I am again convinced that she is a pro. She has definitely done this before. Now even though I am enjoying the work she is doing its 4am and this is not my chick so I won't be staying the night. I need to make this a hit and run session. I move her over to the bed, at this point I'm completely naked and so is she. Her body was gorgeous. Her skin soft, no blemishes a milky tone of light caramel. And of course she had an ass out of this world. Just the sight of her ass made me even harder.

Her breasts were very perky. They sat perfect on her frame. Nice handfuls that with just one look you would want to suck. I'm all over her. My hand's not missing an inch of her body. I lay down on the bed as she continues to give me head.

More and more I'm getting into it, but I am still half focused on the old guy in the corner watching the two of us. I shake it off and relax a little more while she's doing work. The head she gives is good. Although I like head, and believe me I do.

It doesn't blow my mind. The ultimate turn on for me is the idea of pleasing my woman. Giving is what gets me off. Enough of this I grab her waist and move her around. Without missing a beat she keeps the penis in her mouth and sits her pussy right on my lips. I take her clit and begin to tease it with my tongue. From the sideline I hear her husband giving her direction on how to suck my dick. Letting her know that he is enjoying what he sees. Wow, can you imagine telling your wife that you enjoy the work she's doing on another mans cock? Very weird to imagine, its like im caught in a low budget flick or something very similar. Who cares? I'm drunk and this chick has got me going. I make sure to let her know that I am also enjoying the work she is doing.

After teasing and sucking I feel her about to climax. I start sucking harder as she releases a moan that would wake everyone in her neighborhood. Her orgasm was very strong. I am feeling myself right now. With a moan like that she has definitely experienced something different. And if I can make her come with my mouth I know my dick is better. Confirmation comes next. She turns around and sucks the juices from my lips then whispers to me. "Damn that was better than my husband". Now she and I are ready to feel something. She reaches for a condom, I quickly grab my own. I don't know about the rest of you cats but if I don't buy the box I am not using them. She takes the condom and slowly slides it on my cock. I'm throbbing wanting to see what her ride is like. She sits on top of me and slides down on my dick. I'm watching her facial expressions, her eyes closed and mouth open as I'm penetrating her no words needed to let me know she's enjoying how I am filling her up. She begins to grind on me as I take both of her breasts in my hands. I'm squeezing and sucking her nipples soon she begins to grind faster and then bounces up and down on me. I swear after 3 or 4 minutes it begins to feel so good to her I can feel her about to climax again. She's working me so deep and fast I feel every corner inside of her. Grinding me slow and hard I feel her juice all over me soon after that moan again follows.

Her husband sitting on the sideline must be enjoying what he sees I can tell her has begun to jack off. I see his movement from the corner of my eye. After she gets her orgasm I switch positions and lay her on her back. It's my turn! I press her knees to the bed and slowly glide my cock inside her. Again I'm watching her facial expressions as it goes in. Her mouth opens wide as her eyes roll back in her head.

I give her a moment to become used to the feel before digging deep inside of her. I start off slow and then a little faster. Her husband must be really hot right now or feeling left out because he creeps over to the side of the bed adjacent to her head. He gets right up on her and drops his shorts down to the floor. At that moment I focus entirely on her. I really don't want to witness another guys package up close and personal. Right on queue

Dynasty turns her head and takes her husbands cock in her mouth. She's trying hard to maintain but taking his cock in her mouth and mine in her pussy seems a bit too much for her. Then again not many can handle me in bed solo. I'm pounding her harder and deeper all the while that gorgeous face of hers turns blood red. Again it happens, she releases that signature moan of hers and at that point my dick is dripping with her juices.

Now I'm not a greedy man so I turn her over on her knees so that her husband can get a better shot at getting head. Honesty I really don't care if he is enjoying himself I am trying to take full advantage of the opportunity. I grab her waist and begin to do work. I push my cock in her slow and deep making her arch her back so that she can take all of it. I'm beating, she's throwing it back at me. Back and forth it continues. I'm giving it and she's taking all of it trying to maintain while sucking off her husband. I'm thrusting deep inside her. Like a champ going 12 rounds I'm knocking out all sides of her pussy. I'm really feeling myself right now. My stroke is on and this vision of ass before me is turning me on more and more. She's screaming and moaning. Her husband must be pissed off cause she can't keep her mouth closed long enough to perform well for him. This shit is starting to feel too good and I'm not ready to bust just yet so I slow down. I let her control the stroke and pace bouncing back and forth on me. I'm watching her ass bounce up and down. The visual of my dick going in and out of her is enough to make me climax. I feel it coming. I grab her waist and thrust deeper and deeper into her. She must feel me growing inside her because she starts throwing it back hard on me as if she is trying to make me bust. Stroke after stroke its getting closer I cant hold back I'm about to explode. I say fuck it and go with it. I grab both of her ass cheeks and thrust my cock deeper inside of her at that moment it comes. The release was so powerful I thought the condom was about to break. She's grinding on me and tightening her pussy to make the experience even more climatic. I grab her waist and plunge my dick in her. She looks back and smiles as if to say, "job well done".

I'm caught up in the feeling. Damn that shit was good. Though I can't relax cause this isn't my bed or my chick. I'm thinking the party's over and I'm about to get up when she pushing me back down on the bed and climbs on top of me. She looks me in the eye and says, "Now I want to fulfill my fantasy." My eyes open wide with curiosity like damn I thought that's what we just accomplished.

She looks me in the eye and says, "I want you in my pussy while my husband is in my ass." Whoa! This girl is a freak! Willing to do it all without question damn she is a true pro. Not only is she fucking and sucking my brains out, she wants to experience a DP (double penetration). After I got my orgasm I was pretty much done pleasing myself and her but I didn't want to just run out on her when she after all did invite me over to screw her brains out. If it means anything at all I feel sort of obligated at this point to help her fulfill whatever fantasy she had. If it meant giving her more cock I was down. Not to mention I wouldn't mind having her ride me a little while longer. She straddles me and quickly puts my dick inside. Again the look on her face strokes my ego just as well as her pussy strokes my cock. Soon after her husband comes behind her and slides in her ass. I feel her pussy contract a little more as he goes in. He goes in slow as she gasps for a breath of air. After a little bit of wiggling and pushing he's in.

He begins to stroke her ass with a steady pace. She is trying her best to take both of us. To my surprise she takes the dick in her ass about as equally well as the one in her pussy. Again this confirms my belief that this chick is a pro. Damn if it were under different circumstances I may fall for Dynasty. A woman that is willing to go the distance to please her man is hard to come by. And her body on any scale would be a ten with a dime face to match, the perfect combination. What the hell am I thinking? I quickly snap out of that shit. She starts kissing me on my neck and kissing my chest. She looks me in the eye again and thanks me for coming. What could I say except "my pleasure thanks for the invite"? I know its kind of corny but hell what would anybody say in that situation.

After what seems like five minutes her husband is really getting into it. He's pounding her ass and her moans and screams are confirmation enough for him that she is enjoying it. She loves the feel of being penetrated from all sides. He loves it equally as well cause he comes in her ass. The thought of this guy having an orgasm so close to me was a turn off my cock went semi flaccid. He backs away from her and gets his bearings. She grinds on me for a moment then looks at her husband and smiles. He says to her "Happy birthday baby". She replies back, "Thank you baby". Only thing I could think of was yeah-right muthafuckas let me up so I can bounce. You two are some bona-fide freaks. But what does that say about me? I joined in. Who cares? At this point I'm done, Im ready to go. I will sort out all the details later.

Her husband exits im assuming to go to the rest room. That's my queue to leave. She gets off of me and asks me if I enjoyed myself. I don't say a word I just look at her and smile nodding my head. I have only one thing on my mind, leaving her house. I walk to the bathroom picking my cloths off the floor in the process. She follows me into the bathroom and shuts the door behind her. She pushes me against the sink and without saying a word she begins to wash and clean my cock. She takes the soap and towel from the sink and gently washes me. Smiling the entire time she doesn't say a word. Those thoughts of falling for her creep slowly back into my head. I immediately squash that shit and come back to reality. After cleansing my cock she begins to kiss my neck and strike my cock up and down with both hands. After a moment of seduction she goes down on her knees and does work again.

Although it's late as hell and I have my homeboy Ralph in the car waiting I can't help but to allow her to finish what she started. She goes to work fast with her lips, tongue, and hands. It feels so good after about 5 minutes I'm coming in her mouth. I come so strong I could feel it hitting the back of her throat. She takes it out and the rest of my load lands on her face and lips. She doesn't flinch or back away from it at all. She looks at me and smiles. She takes my cock in her hands and wipes the remaining juice from it on her lips. Licking her lips clean she then swallows every drop. Oh my God it was so nasty yet so beautiful all at once. She gets off her knees and walks out of the bathroom. I take a moment to get myself together before coming out of the bathroom myself.

I come out and Dynasty sits on the bed an exhausted look on her face. After tonight I'm sure she is very exhausted. Her husband sits in the corner. I pick up the rest of my things from the floor and he comes over to me. He shakes my hand again and tells me thank you for coming. I'm somewhat thrown by all the gratitude. I have never been thanked so much for screwing someone's wife in front of them. He proceeds to walk me to the door Dynasty waves goodbye and winks at me. I walk out of the room not knowing who came out on top here. Was it them or me? Was I the user or the used? After her husband walks me to the door I tell him to have a great night before hurriedly walking to my car and getting the hell out of dodge. I drive off wake my homeboy's sleepy ass up and say to myself "damn, what a fucking night."

Exchange Of Love

Navarro Love

I will give you my body baby, if you'll give yours.

I'll do anything you ask, even get down on all fours

Can I caress your mind my love, be4 we commit this sin.

This is how a love affair should always begin.

Can I whisper to you my intentions starting with a kiss?

Slowly rolling my tongue, teasing your lips.

If ever there were a time to plead, baby yours is now.

Because once I have my mind around you, there's no coping out.

I will give my heart to you, if you promise to keep it safe.

Because many women have hurt me, leaving my heart raped.

Raped of all it has to give, but only a fraction of what its worth.

Now you're about to receive a taste, a sample sweeter than syrup.

What a word to describe my love, I know baby but its true.

The sweet succulent rich and thick flow, now do you see the nature

of its use?

Honey I wont talk about all the things I will do, once inside of you.

But there will be so many screams from your lips, many you've

never heard

And we shall rewrite the Kama Sutra, but with half as many words.

Baby I wish to exchange with you a great many things,

Most of all my spirit, for in your eyes "heaven"

I have seen.

Love You Betta

Navarro Love

Baby I can love you betta
So much betta than he
I can show you many things
And bring color to your fantasies
I can turn your soul out
And leave your body weak
Can I meet you in ecstasy
And come all over your dreams
Baby trust if he cant make you come
Then I surely can
I can love you better baby
Come try this man

Orgasm

Navarro Love

I'm the object of your desire

men and women alike

When I come I burn with fire

But that match you must strike

So many people long for me

because I'm such a good friend

I will twist you in and out,

to my will you must bend

I will never disappoint you

If given the proper release

Sometimes I can arrive early

With just a simple tease

When I flow hard

I invoke God's name

For those who have never felt my power

I bid you much shame

I am the alpha and omega

The reason for your sexual urge

I can always visit you while your alone

But I'm best after she's got hers

G-Spot

Navarro Love

Can you find me hiding?
Do you feel me there?
To reach me you must go deeper
Perhaps with her legs in the air
Although I am more assessable from behind
I know its frustrating trying to find
I'm the spot that makes her love come down
So intense is the river's flow
If you really want to find me,
how far are you willing to go?
If you touch me I will give,
pleasure greater than your wildest dreams
Soft and moist my composition
Yet to most I am seldom seen
I am here for you waiting,
to be discovered by your touch
If you believe in me you will find
Once found after me you will lust
I am lost inside you
I am the spot that makes your body run hot
I'm a part of you like no other
I am known as the g-spot.

You Want Me

Navarro Love

I see you staring, wondering could this be

Lost within a trance

The very essence of a man stands before thee

I've seen you watching, as I've had my eyes on you

If I approached and said hello, I'm sure of what you would do

Quickly ask my name and I shall do the same

Dispelling all thoughts of un-approachability, yes,

I see that you want me

As I give you the look, that has left so many shook

Trembling inside you try hard to hide your smile

But for sure my shit has got you

Like the sands of an hourglass you slowly start to pass

Into the realm to which I reign supreme

Can you imagine my kiss, nothing short of bliss

Just a taste and you will see, that yes, you want me

Like a classic old school joint, my love gets better with time

And I know that you long for a sample

With the body of a goddess, my cup you can surely fill

Because from my eyes it's more than ample

If you bathe in the rain you still wouldn't be as wet

Trust you surely wont forget

And as sure as there is sand in the sea,

Baby, I know you want me

SEX

Navarro Love

It consumes my mind, constantly calling me
I try to shake it off but I feel your hands
touching me
Sometimes I even think there's something
wrong with me
I see it at night its forever in my dreams
Is it wrong for me to think of it at work
Or when your sitting next to me listening
to the sermon at church
Baby I cant help it,
it's your body that I crave
Even on holiest of days
The sex we have leaves me in an
orgasmic rage
Please don't say to me, that I
cant have what I want
Can you hear me calling out to your body
And I want to keep you forever
at the tip of my tongue

What If

Navarro Love

2day I heard a whisper, one spoken with a kiss

Imagine if you will, that kiss was upon your lips,

Oh my love, what if

What if I sang 2 you,

in a language that only you and I could hear

A sweet serenade for winds

that would even surpass Mozart's gift

Oh my love, what if.

What if you were to awake each morning in my arms,

the same arms that protected you while u slept.

In this game of chance I have lost my dear

Because of the cards you've dealt

Am I a fool to think of such things, a man lost or insane?

But a beautiful picture you are my love

and I wish to be your frame.

Oh my love, what if I could capture the stars for u,

and move mountains with the love we make,

I know it would be wonderful, a 7.9 quake

The other 1.1 spent caressing you, holding you till we awake.

Baby what if you and I meant YOU AND I?

Would that make u happy?

Would u smile each day you live?

What if my love, oh baby, what if

One Hit Wonder

Navarro Love

Baby was it good enough for you?

Cause it was damn good to me

Thought I was convinced by your screams,

but I hadn't heard from you in a week.

Thought maybe it was something I did, or maybe something I said

All sorts of visions ran through my head

Could it be another lover put it down, even more so than my thunder?

Hell I know it was a mighty spell, the experience I put you under.

The rhythm of my hips, and flick of my tongue so superb

So why hasn't she called, why not even one word.

I know my shit was good,

as attested by many lovers in my past

But yet with you I am alone, why no call I ask

After that night I spent with you I was sure that whatever we create

No one in this world could put asunder

Or maybe I've just fell victim, to being a one hit wonder.

Reunion

Navarro Love

I shiver when I think of being inside you
Our reunion of lovemaking is
well over due
Bring only your desires to bed,
your body and no clothes
Let me lose myself inside you
While navigating your black hole
Exploring places unknown,
or at least known only to you
There's no limit to where we can go
my love
No limit to what I will do
Reconnect with me, and lets make it
better than the last
A shame to compete with perfection
but now we must record a new past
Baby I shiver,
when I think of being inside you
Our reunion of lovemaking is well
overdue

Can You Picture

Navarro Love

Candle light baby just you and me,
2night is the night we act upon your fantasies.
None recycled baby these were made for us
Nothing is forbidden while we're making love.
Picture a silhouette of you and I
Envision if you will my head between your thighs
The soft wet caress of the buds on my tongue
Its okay baby if it feels good, just this once you can cum.
Now picture my body
This perfect specimen of what a man should look like
With no desire other than your world, I long to be inside.
Your warm dark world that consumes my love
as I thrust deep inside
Just for the night? No my love, I want to last a lifetime.
For this picture we create is too beautiful to erase,
Even when making love, I still fantasize.
Can you picture how love is supposed to feel?
Or the true definition of Orgasm
It starts with a deep pulsating pressure, then suddenly an
explosion, too much feeling words cant fathom
Then picture the longing embrace after we're through
Silence as our eyes connect, and I whisper
"I Love You"

Monogamy

Navarro Love

For so long you have been my lady

But tonight please be my whore

There's so many things left to discover

Our bodies, let's fully explore

There's nothing I want more,

than to truly please you

I'll do whatever you say, baby I'm your slave

Use me, don't hold back anymore

Handcuffs or toys baby there's so

many things we can enjoy

For it's with monogamy that I'm loving you

And you hold the key to

what's locked behind that door.

Virginity

Navarro Love

So long ago it seems that I lost you,

maybe at the age of fourteen

At times I wish you were still with me

My new friend Sex has turned me into a fiend

My addiction soon took hold, no longer was I in control

Virginity where can you be

Each time it becomes scarier

I need you to save me

Bless me with purity as I once had before

For those days are long past,

With the many lovers that have walked out my door

I try to stay focused and safe at all times

though it's hard not having you by my side

I keep my head held high

as to not look back to the past

Sometimes I wish I kept you with me

my old friend Virginity

Emphasis On Sex

Navarro Love

People place so much emphasis on sex

What about making love?

No radio playing, making love to the sound of the rain,

that's what love is made of

Does it always have to be a hit and run?

Baby lets take our time.

I want to spend the night with you tonight

Just to let you know your mine

I'm tired of the fuck songs lets play some Luther V.

Or maybe a little Isley Brothers, and end with Teddy p.

Marvin said it best,

I want you, the right way

So lets not waste another moment let's start from today

There's so much emphasis on sex

You even see it on the horror flick screens

I'd rather take my time and make love to you

And only in my bed will you scream

What That Booty Do

Navarro Love

Am I wrong to use the word fuck,

to describe what you do to me?

Damn you blow my mind, ecstasy this must be.

Sometimes though I wonder,

was it done on another?

Because your skills are too advanced,

for me to be your first lover

Baby you put my mind at ease, each time with that thing you

do

Everyday I can't wait to be alone with you

I want to see what that booty do.

Again my mind draws back,

I wonder whose using who?

Am I the one getting over?

Who else has seen what that booty do?

Show me again, the object of my affection

In those tight little jeans you wear

You give me an instant erection

And each day I cant wait, until I can be alone with you

Please say you'll show me again

I want to see what that booty do.

One Night Alone With You
(Verbal Tease)

Come here baby, I've been waiting on you. Can we sit here by the fire while I hold you next to me? I want to watch the light of the flame dance across your beautiful face. It's like a hand caressing your cheek and gently touching your lips. Baby I've waited for this day for so long it's been in my dreams. Lay your head across my lap and any song you choose I will sing. Can I play in your long flowing hair while I feed you strawberries and cream? Let me kiss and lick the juice from your lips.

Your touch makes it sweeter still. Now lay in front of the fire and I will lie on your back. I will massage your body with mine missing not one inch. All your timid fears will disappear after your second glass of wine. Or maybe this red passion Alize will be enough to ease your mind. For tonight I belong only to you, and yes you are all mine. I have thought of your touch, your feel, and kiss many times over. Baby I can't wait any longer. Tonight is not about sex, it's about exploring the beauty of you. My mind is fixed, and I prayed to have this one night alone with you. (2 be continued)

The Greatest Sex

Imagine if you will, we have just finished making love.
We've just shared each other's bodies in the most intimate of ways.
We lay in silence drenched in sweat looking into each other's eyes,
wondering what the other is thinking. Imagine yourself lying there
naked. My figure in front of you, staring back at you with only the
light of the moon shining through your bedroom window. No
music playing, no candles burning, just silence only the beating of
our hearts make a sound. It seems as if we stare into each other's
eyes for an hour before saying a word. Then all of a sudden I say,
"Come closer to me". You move closer to me and our hands touch.
I take your hand in mine and look deeper in your eyes.

Together we witness what few have. Many thoughts begin
to race through our minds, our future, the past, your today, our
tomorrow. You begin to wonder what's next. What can another day
together bring for you and I? The physical attraction surpassed we
have just reached a moment where our minds have connected way
beyond my lady, and I your man. Although our sex was good, our
exchange of the mind was better. No lustful thoughts it's so pure.
We have just opened ourselves to accept the greatest sex of all. A
spiritual bond an engagement of our souls. Now with each touch
what we share it is magnified. Your senses are heightened and
your mind aroused. From this moment on when we make love, we
do with our souls and minds. Our bodies will follow suit. There's
no limit, no boundaries, no end. Open your mind to me and let

your conscience be free. Make love to me as if I were you and you were me. What would you want me to experience if I were you? If you cannot fathom then you are not truly free. Baby let go, and enjoy me as if I were you. And I shall do the same. And when we awake in the morning. We shall begin again. Rewriting the love we share and the sex we make enough to fill volumes of books. It's the greatest sex, not of the body but that of the mind. Experience it with me. Experience us experience me.

Chapter 3

Pain

My Pain vs. My Happiness

My pain exists. All of us carry this weight called pain in whatever form it manifests itself. Some the pain for a lover lost, or a lost loved one. For others that ever so illusive word called happiness. What creates your pain? What makes you happy? I guess if we could answer these questions none of us would be without happiness. If we walked day to day happy would we appreciate it still? Without the feeling of pain none would understand or know the true nature of how happiness makes us feel. But is pain a reflection of what doesn't bring us happiness or just a void within the mind. Possibly a void we are trying to fill for all the wrong reasons, with all the wrong substitutes. We can ask do those substitutes really bring us joy or just ease the pain and allow us to forget what makes us sad. My joy, my pain, my happiness, my sorrow, can all be summed with one word. That word is "life".

What does life mean to you? What means the world to you? Is it that job you have been wanting for years? Is it that sports car that just came out that you can't wait to put rims on? Is it watching your child take its first step? What is it about, this word called life? If life means forever why does it end? So many questions but who has the answers? When you take a step back and reflect on life and your existence on this earth can you say that "Yes, I accomplished all that I set out to do". Can you say that the pain you endured through life helped you reach your plateau of happiness? We all search for that plain, that euphoric place called happiness. The steps we all take to get there are not so different from the next. We laugh, we cry, we sing, we dance, all in an effort to find peace. All in an effort to wake up and one day say, "I am truly happy". Some say with money comes happiness. Is that true? How many of us truly believe that money is the end all be all to utopia? Some say it brings more problems. Well if money can't buy you happiness, it surely can pay for the search.

My pain exists. It has many forms. It is far reaching very complex. Each of us carries a weight of pain. Understanding it and taking control is what brings about happiness. Pain is never ending for it will always be with you. But through pain comes an abundance of happiness. Seek it and let it flow.

A Mans Cry

Navarro Love
(Dedicated to all black males)

Somebody wake me cause its terrifying sleeping

So many demons in my dreams got a nigga screaming

Still I wake up with a chip on my shoulder

I can't explain it but my heart is getting colder

I got a lady that's ready to raise a family, but I can't see myself

taking care of somebody else's seed.

On my knees everyday begging the Lord to save me

Cause if I die and he wont I know the devil will take me.

Everything I do in life, I just try to be a better man

But it's kinda hard when loneliness and life go hand in hand.

I'm crying out with my heart, somebody's got to hear

But with each scream I feel my time of death is drawing near.

Is it fair to say that I lived a troubled life

I don't know cause many would give anything to be me for one

night.

So much pressure and strain that's not the way to live

But if I felt love, would I know if that love was real.

I was born of you God and to you I return.

Just please have a place for me, your wayward son

I don't want to die but if I go, I will go with ease

Cause this burden of life I deal, was only meant for me.

Mama Why U Cry

Navarro Love

As a young boy I often wonder why
I would always see tears in my mothers' eyes
Was it something I've done?
Did I not bring you joy?
I know everybody needs love,
but what about loving your baby boy
If I could I would give you the world
Even with infant eyes I adored
You were always my favorite girl.
Why do you search for love so wicked?
So many nights hearing you cry
left my mind twisted
Crying inside all the while adorning a smile
Mama I love you, tell me why you cry
Why does your heart wear a frown?

My Shattered World

Navarro Love

My world was shattered the moment
I watched you cry.
Those tears I tried to erase,
with my lips I tried to dry.
But it was I that created the sorrow
trapped within you heart
Your pain unimaginable,
how I tore your world apart.
Baby I'm sorry for my insecurities,
everything I did was for selfish reasons
Still your heart remained true
Tell me how do I make it better
How do I make lovebirds sing
throughout this stormy weather?
My world was shattered, the moment I made you cry.
That moment I saw a part of me die
Looking deep within your eyes.

A Woman Scorn

Navarro Love

Why must I be a prisoner of the mind?
So many un-truths so many words unkind
Believed in that which I held true
Believed so much in you
Now you say that you don't want me,
but my friend will suffice
I'd give my blood to prevent that
Would that be the ultimate sacrifice?
This pain is unbearable, piercing my heart
like a dull edged sword
Its true hell hath no fury,
like a woman scorn

Bitch

Navarro Love

I should've never let you inside my heart,
I should've known you were a Bitch!
I didn't know you'd tare my world apart and leave, you fucking
Bitch!
Selfish is the only way to describe you,
how could you ask for anything more
I gave my all and dreams to you, and you raped them like a whore.
Lies and games and on you still a smile remained
Knowing that all the while an agenda was your ticket to fame.
How can I explain my hurt and pain in fewer words than 6.
I can sum it all up in just a few words, you sorry Bitch!
Tell me who are you putting your mouth on now,
Whose cigarette are you smoking?
You do it oh so well, without any discrimination or choking.
But I hope love leaves a nasty taste in your mouth, one
that's well worth loathing.
I cared and released tears for you,
and now another penis you're holding
Once the ride stopped and it was all said and done
the true Bitch came out in you.
So if you think I'm disrespecting you, dumb BITCH I am
And I just want to say fuck your boy, your family, and your friends
I should've never been your man

Missing You

Navarro Love

Its been five years, and still I cant let go
Of the day you left me, and your voice
I would hear no more
I wish so much just to feel your touch again
From my beginning you were there
You wanted nothing more than to be around your boy
You watched your son grow into a man
Some nights I sit and cry,
wondering if I make you proud.
My regret is you will not be here,
to help me raise my first child
Grandmother I'm missing you
More than your baby boy can say
I'm so lost without you here
This pain grows stronger everyday
If I could express my love for you in words,
the sweetest song I would write for you
Incomplete is my state without you,
like this planet without the moon
For no other reason my grandmother
But I am missing you

These Tears Of Mine

Navarro Love

How many tears must I shed before light shines on my heart?

So many scares from this war with love so hard fought.

Some say it's cleansing, it washes away your pain,

For that I would need my tears to flow like rain.

That's all that I have left now, these tears of mine.

Once I thought I found happiness, the one that would stand throughout time.

Am I wrong to wish for such things, if it's not to be?

I don't know, I couldn't tell, so many tears I can't see.

If they could talk to me I wonder what they would say.

For I carry them with me constantly, they are with me at night and before I wake.

Is it possible to cry while your asleep, maybe I am alone in my dreams?

No tracks needed to bare witness to me crying, for my tears run like streams.

A fool for crying some might say, but I'd be a fool if I didn't.

Nonetheless I keep a façade, my true feelings left hidden.

I wonder how many more breaks this small heart can take

Before I am left with just a shell

But until then I am left only with these tears of mine

To know the pain I feel, look close for in my eyes they always tell.

Solo

Navarro Love

So low nothing beneath me

the curb is a giant.

Happiness a mountain,

with the highest peak

So low even my dreams in silence,

my laughter has no sound.

The coldest depths of space I dwell

my darkness abound.

So low I can truly fathom,

the depths of the sea.

So low I can imagine

a world where the population is

me

She Said Tomorrow

Navarro Love

She said, I will give my love to you

But with a busted heart what can anyone do?

Depression and understatement, left tattered and torn

With each lover that's come my way

a scar was left.

She sings a song of a woman scorn.

I will give my love to you tomorrow

For today is not worth the heartache and sorrow

A woman with baggage I am, my heart so borrowed.

Why give my love today when you can have me

tomorrow?

I say tomorrow is too far away.

All your dark days are done.

So accept my love today

for tomorrow may never come.

Politics of Pain
Navarro Love

Dear Mr. President you say you want me to stand

Stand for a system that rarely believes in me

Hard for me to buy a home, no food to eat

While thousands of miles away my brother is dying for free

What's the cost of freedom?

Would it be my rights and privacy?

Tapping my phone, reading my mail

But you want me to stand for you

and send another man to hell

If I say no, in this country you say I don't belong

So many in New Orleans lost without family,

left without a home

What am I to do when the price of death costs less than

living?

Maybe I should just blow my brains out and stop dealing

If that's what you're selling, sorry I'm not buying

But for your sickness I have a cure, that's well over due

I will exercise my right to raise my right hand

and say fuck you!

Stained

Navarro Love

I write this to eliminate and erase you from my being

Hoping that when this ink runs out so will this empty feeling

I write this to record the pain, the pain of my heart stained

Stained with the poison of love and hope,

hell where's the love high?

Thought it was more potent than dope

I write this to get you out of my mind,

some say it will just take time

To feel again like I'm on top.

Damn will this ink ever stop?

This Game

Navarro Love

I count the days and hours since you left

So many not wanting to take a breath

The foolishness of this game, please I don't want to play

But this bed I made with you, now I must lay.

Lie only with my sorrow and the seclusion of a heart at last alone

Baby I would give or do anything to make this house a home

The truth you say you want.

Damn that's asking a bit much

But each day a part of me dies, without feeling your touch

My angel I treated you so wrong

So much I know was my fault

But never would I have done those things

If this were the end result

A resolution with you I seek, baby take a picture

I cant imagine what your doing now,

and all the things he's doing with you

How could you believe those lies?

That playa was my claim to fame.

Baby I am much wiser now,

I don't want to play this game

These Dreaming Eyes Of Mine

Navarro Love

I dream of heaven, I dream of the sea

I dream of a morning, when I awake I smile

Instead I awake and cannot remember

my mind filled with clouds

I dream of contentment a place of piece

Day after day I search not wanting to believe

That it exists only in my dreams

I dream of a place where a touch gives sight to the blind

Can you see what I see?

Through these dreaming eyes of mine

I Hate U

Navarro Love

I hate you, more than I've hated anyone else
I hate you for the love I gave till I had nothing left
You ask why do I hate you?
So many ways to count
Maybe it's for the countless lies
Or the many friends you've had in your mouth
I hate you baby some would call it love
If love makes you hate this much
Then what exactly is love made of?

About You

Navarro Love

These few words are for you no name is due

Once read you will understand, you will know the truth

You love nothing, by your actions not even yourself

A constant game of playing and lies

I know you have another man,

I've felt it between your thighs

Why do you damage yourself so?

Do you aspire to be the world's next top ho?

Even still I get caught up

What's this man to do?

As you read you can see,

that these words are about you

I Know

Navarro Love

I know I was a fool, to ever let you leave

I know the drama that was caused, all stemmed from me

A playa in training I didn't quite know the rules

Now I sit in a vip section reserved for fools

I can hear the laughter of those that witnessed what I lost

My dreams are nightmares, a horror flick not worth the cost

All the sorrows in the world cant bring my old reality back

And this hard lesson I have learned

Now that it's over

Can anyone tell me how I can begin to let it burn?

Emotional

Navarro Love

I try to hide how I feel
but my face cannot mask
The many pains I feel when thinking of you
and the memories of our past
I can't let go, I've tried but my heart can tell
That my mind is lost within you,
your memory is my cell
Never again will I see or hear,
your face or voice when I awake
Damn just the thought of knowing you,
maybe it was a mistake
Long days locked in my room thinking of you
tell me how do I forget
Its hell living without you
the word Emotional fails to project
But caught up in you I am,
deep this jones has got me
I keep a smile while dying inside
Someone please set me free

Conclusion

So now that we have come to the end, what road will you take? Again this is not a book of poetry but yet a conversation piece. When you are on your journey through life and relationships and there is a fork in that road, which road will you take? The one that leads to love, the one that leads to sex, or will you sabotage everything and continue the cycle of pain? We all have choices nothing is done by happen stance. Everything thing is of free will.

We must understand the nature of ourselves as we try to understand others. In understanding yourself you break down the false barriers you've created and begin to fully understand how our actions affect others. The most powerful tool in a relationship is understanding how you affect someone else. In doing so you can create a bond so strong that know one can break not even yourself. Open your eyes to what realism has in store for you. Knowing others is to know yourself. My pain exists, but so does my love. If sex is your addiction true happiness is the cure. Seek it out the right way. Love God, love life, and experience a love like no other a Love Burgundy.

Navarro Love

THANK U's

God, no words needed to express.
Mother, a simple thank u fails to comprehend exactly what you have done.
Brother, thank you for your guidance.
Chuck Blue, thank you for helping me throw them hands when we were kids I'm always here for you cuz.
My sis, I love you
To all those who have pushed me to let the world experience my work, thank you.
To that guy in Minneapolis, your inspiration is golden. Thank You. You are truly the G.O.A.T.

NAVARIA
Productions

Visit Us

facebook/NavariaEnterprises

Twitter @NavariaEnt

NavariaEnterprises@gmail.com

Also Available

Loves Epiphany

Novel
by
Navarro Love

Thank you and we hope you've enjoyed your journey.

Ne
NAVARIA ENTERPRISES

www.ingramcontent.com/pod-product-compliance
Lightning Source LLC
Chambersburg PA
CBHW060140050426

42448CB00010B/2224